Full Bloom

Full Bloom

VIBRANT PLANT-BASED RECIPES
FOR YOUR SUMMER TABLE

Virpi Mikkonen

Creator of Vanelja.com

NewSeed
PRESS

Contents

Morning

Daytime

Sweet

Wellness

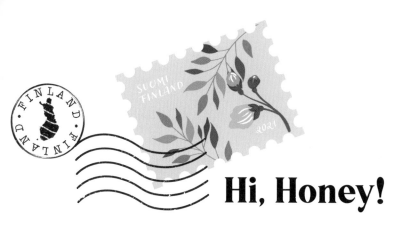

Hi, Honey!

WELCOME TO *FULL BLOOM*! I wrote this book for you to enjoy the summer season's vibrant smells, tastes, sights, sounds, and textures; to take full advantage of nature's beautiful buffet; to glow inside and out; and, most importantly, to eat healthy and locally. For me, beauty is one-half of the entire eating experience, and I love to create nuanced tastes that make for truly unforgettable recipes—and summer is the perfect season for doing just that! With fresh vegetables, herbs, fruits, and flowers bursting with energy and color, I've included my family's favorite summer recipes that always make us smile. Nature and Nordic traditions are always close to my heart. I was born and raised in Finland, a Nordic country between Sweden and Russia, so you'll find lots of Finnish- and Scandinavian-inspired recipes in the following pages that use lots of fresh berries, oats, and wild herbs. As you will see, the ingredients are simple, authentic, bright, and cheerful. They not only taste incredibly delicious but also will make you proud to serve to friends and family. I truly believe that if a dish makes you happy upon first sight, the rest of the meal is an assured success!

For many of the recipes, I include easy tips to take advantage of the abundant treasures summer offers us: wild herbs and flowers! When I walk outdoors during the summertime, I always grab something on my path, such as wild rose petals, dandelion leaves, birch buds, or clover flowers. This book gives you suggestions on how to bring the outdoors to your indoor table. Since it is said that we are what we eat, why not eat everything beautiful and vibrant?

Finally, I also share some of my summer-inspired body and skin wellness recipes with you. There is nothing more relaxing than foraging fresh ingredients for pampering foot soaks, fragrant face mists, or sweet honey masks. After all, life is to be enjoyed, and there is no better time to enjoy it than during the summer. I wish you a beautiful summer season full of delicious, summery tastes and sights on your plates.

Stay wild, summer's child!

♥ Virpi

Morning

Baked Apple & Oat Slices

These baked apples slices with oat crumble topping are an easy-and-quick luxurious dish made with super basic ingredients.

Makes 9-12 slices

3 sweet apples
1 cup (9 oz/250 g) oat-based yogurt
½ cup (1¾ oz/50 g) rolled oats
½ cup (1¾ oz/50 g) almond flour
   (or oat flour)
½ tsp baking powder
1 tsp ground ceylon cinnamon
2 tbsp coconut sugar
Vanilla ice cream (or yogurt), for serving

Preheat the oven to 400°F (200°C) and line a baking sheet with parchment paper. Cut the apples in half and remove the seeds. Cut the apples lengthwise into ½-inch (12-mm) slices. In a medium bowl, combine the yogurt, oats, almond flour, baking powder, and cinnamon. Spread the apple slices on the prepared baking sheet. Take a big spoonful of the oat crumble mixture and spread it evenly on top of each apple slice. Sprinkle each evenly with the coconut sugar. Bake for 20–25 minutes until golden. Let cool for about 10 minutes until they firm up. Place the slices on serving plates with a spatula. Serve slightly warm with a scoop of vanilla ice cream.

Tip! Enjoy the apple slices for breakfast with yogurt or as a dessert with some ice cream. Try it with fresh berries.

Summer Berry Oatmeal

This *berrylicious* oatmeal is a sweet
and summery breakfast that
can be enjoyed both warm or cold.

Serves 1

BERRY PURÉE
¼ cup (1¼ oz/35 g) blueberries
¼ cup (1½ oz/40 g) black currants
¼ cup (1 oz/30 g) raspberries
1–2 tsp local organic honey
  (or maple syrup)

OATMEAL
1½ cups oat milk (or half oat milk,
  half water)
1 cup (3½ oz/100 g) rolled oats
½ tsp ground cardamom
Pinch sea salt

TOPPINGS
Sunflower seeds
Pumpkin seeds
Oat milk

To prepare the berry purée, blend the blueberries, black currants, raspberries, and honey in a blender. To prepare the oatmeal, pour the oat milk into a pot and bring to a boil. Add the oats and cook over medium heat for 5 minutes. Cover and leave to simmer on low heat for 5 more minutes. Stir in cardamon, salt, and a couple of spoonfuls of berry purée. Taste and adjust the sweetness with more honey or a sweetener. Pour into a serving bowl, top with berry purée, add the toppings of choice, and enjoy.

Tip! You can substitute the berries in this recipe with any berry that is in season.

Detox Herb Juice

If you feel like you might not be getting enough greens, make this strengthening juice a daily habit.

Serves 1

2 celery ribs
½ cucumber
1 apple
½ lemon
Handful baby spinach
Handful parsley
3 kale leaves
1-inch (2.5 cm) slice fresh ginger

Rinse and cut all ingredients into smaller pieces to fit in juicer. Prepare the juice with your juicer. Enjoy right away. Store in a sealed bottle in the refrigerator and use within 24 hours.

Tip! If you don't own a juicer, blend the ingredients in a blender with a small splash of water until fully pureed and strain the juice with cheesecloth or a sieve.

Golden Glow Bircher Muesli

Here comes the sun! Bircher muesli is a nourishing and fulfilling breakfast with sunshine vibes.

Serves 3

1 cup (9 oz/250 g) natural coconut yogurt
   (or other natural yogurt)
1 cup (8 fl oz/240 ml) rice milk
   (or oat-based milk)
1 cup (3 oz/90 g) Bircher muesli
   (or overnight oats or buckwheat flakes)
1 apple, grated
¼ cup (1½ oz/40 g) raisins
2 tbsp chopped pecans
2 tbsp almond flakes
1 tsp local organic honey or maple syrup
1 tbsp orange juice
1 tsp ground turmeric
½ tsp ground cinnamon
½ tsp ground cardamom
Pinch ground black pepper
Petals from 3 dandelion flowers (optional)

TOPPINGS
Nuts, seeds, berries, and/or fruit of choice
Dandelion, rose, and/or lilac petals

Combine all the ingredients except the toppings in a large bowl or jar. Set overnight in the refrigerator. Enjoy with nuts, seeds, berries, and fruits of choice. Raspberry, mango, and orange are a great match here!

Tip! Bircher muesli was first created in the early 1900s by Swiss doctor Maximilian Bircher-Benner. There are countless varieties of muesli, and it's very easy to make. Soak raw oats overnight in milk with fruits and nuts. Be sure to try different seeds, grains, and fruits.

Rhubarb Rose Cordial

Rhubarb juice is a summer classic,
which I like to flavor with wild rose petals.

Serves 5

64 fl oz (2 l) water

4 cups (900 g/32 oz) rhubarb , cut to
 small pieces

2 cups (approx. 80 petals) wild rose petals

Juice of 1 lemon

½ cup (3½ oz/100 g) erythritol

Combine all the ingredients in a large pot and bring to a boil. Let simmer on low heat for 15 minutes. Take off the heat and let stand for 1 hour. Strain the juice into large, clean bottles. Store in the refrigerator and use within a week.

Tip! You can switch the sweeter in this recipe with xylitol or coconut sugar; just keep in mind that with a darker sweetener you will get a darker cordial.

Vanilla-Pear Chia Pudding

Chia puddings are a nourishing yet light option for a summer breakfast or snack. Be sure to be generous and garnish with berries and nuts.

Serves 1-2

1 cup (8 fl oz/240 ml) rice milk
2 pears
½ tsp vanilla extract (or vanilla powder)
½ tsp ground cardamom
3 tbsp chia seeds

Measure all the ingredients except chia seeds into a blender and blend until smooth. Pour into a jar or small bowl and stir in the chia seeds. Leave to thicken for 10 minutes. Stir again and place in the refrigerator overnight (or for at least 1 hour).

Tip! A great ingredient to improve digestive health, chia seeds contain lots of fiber, protein, omega-3 fatty acids, and several minerals and antioxidants, so they make a great addition to your diet. Chia seeds absorb water and fat, so use them to thicken soups, sauces, smoothies, and jams, or use them as an egg substitute by combining 1 tablespoon of chia seeds with 2½ tablespoons of water, mixing and allowing to thicken for 10 minutes.

Dandelion

Dandelion is a powerful herb that is full of vitamins, and yet it's quite rarely used. Young dandelion leaves are perfect additions to salads, soups, and stews. Since dandelion flowers are edible, they can be a colorful and unexpected garnish on top of salads and desserts or blended into lattes and smoothies. Try cooking dandelion flower buds and roots in slightly salted water and enjoy them as a side dish. I eat three to five dandelion flowers a day during the summer for a burst of vibrant, sunshiny energy.

Sunshine Spread

This highly nutritious spread pairs perfectly with bread and bagels. Be sure to add some avocado, fresh herbs, or cherry tomatoes as a garnish!

Makes about 1 ½ cups (12 oz/340 g)

1¼ cups (7½ oz/210 g) chickpeas
  (cooked or canned)
⅓ cup (2½ oz/70 g) chopped sun-dried
  tomatoes
¼ cup (1 oz/30 g) cashews, soaked
  for 30 minutes
1 clove garlic
Juice of ½ lemon
2 tbsp olive oil
5 fresh basil leaves
Pinch sea salt
Pinch ground black pepper
5 tbsp (2½ fl oz/75 ml) tbsp fresh water
Petals from 3 dandelion flowers
Around 20 bagels

TOPPINGS
Sliced avocado
Fresh herbs
Bean sprouts
Radishes
Cherry tomatoes

Place all the ingredients except the toppings in a blender and blend until nice and smooth. Add more water, as needed, to obtain your desired consistency. Taste and add salt and pepper as needed. Store in the refrigerator in a sealed jar and use within a week. Spread on toast or bagels and top with the vegetables and herbs of your choice.

Tip! One of my favorite summer toasts includes this spread, avocado slices, cherry tomatoes, sliced radish, sprouts, and lots of fresh basil. Parsley and cilantro work great with this combination. When it comes to fresh herbs, more is more for me!

3-Ingredient Crêpes

Not only are these crêpes super easy to make, once filled with yogurt and berries—voilà—breakfast is served! A salty filling goes really well with them.

Makes about 8 crêpes

1 cup (3½ oz/100 g) rolled oats
1 cup (8 fl oz/240 ml) oat milk
1 large organic egg (or 1 tbsp ground
 flaxseed)

FILLING
Yogurt (or whipped coconut cream
or oat whip)
Banana slices
Peanut butter
Berries of choice

Place the oats, oat milk, and egg in a blender and blend until smooth. Leave to thicken for 10 minutes and then blend again. Heat a nonstick griddle or pan on medium heat. Keep a big spoon beside you. Pour about ¼ cup (2 fl oz/60 ml) of batter into the pan and quickly spread with the spoon to create a thin crêpe. Cook for about 1½ minutes until the surface looks a bit dry. Flip and cook the other side. Repeat with the remaining batter. To stuff the crêpes, spread the filling of your choice in the center. Fold the sides to create a roll. Enjoy!

Spruce Sprout Smoothie

This smoothie is my favorite way to enjoy spruce sprouts (also known as spruce buds), which are the immune-boosting, annual growth parts of spruce trees.

Serves 2

2 tbsp spruce sprouts (about 30 pieces)
2 apples, peeled and cored
1 avocado, pitted and peeled
Juice of 1 lime
2 cups (16 fl oz/475 ml) oat milk

Place all the ingredients in a blender and blend until smooth. Serve with ice cubes or blend some ice cubes into the smoothie to make it extra fresh.

Tip! You can substitute spruce buds with spruce needles, but make sure that your blender is strong enough to break down the spruce needles fully to ensure there are no sharp needles in the smoothie.

Spruce Sprouts

Spruce sprouts are my favorite wild herb to use in the springtime. Pick the light green buds from spring to early summer when they are still soft. They work great in smoothies, salads, and stews. Sprinkle them on top of any dish or enjoy them raw. I personally like to eat them as they are, fresh from the evergreen tree, and I also freeze them to use in the winter. Try steeping them in hot water for a lovely tea. Spruce buds are also a nutritious spice when ground in a coffee grinder. You will need a permission from the landowner to pick spruce sprouts.

Summer Banana Bread

Strawberries paired with banana bread is a match made in summer heaven. Strawberry chia jam and peanut butter are the perfect finishing touches.

Makes 1 loaf / Serves around 5

Coconut oil, to grease loaf pan
2 tbsp ground flaxseed + 5 tbsp
    (2½ fl oz/75 ml) water (or 2 large
    organic eggs)
3 ripe bananas, smashed
½ cup (4 fl oz/120 ml) oat milk
2 cups (7 oz/200 g) almond flour
1 cup (3½ oz/100 g) rolled oats
1½ tbsp ground ceylon cinnamon
½ tsp ground cardamom
½ tsp vanilla powder
¼ tsp sea salt
1 tsp baking powder
2 tbsp coconut sugar
1 cup fresh strawberries, cut to
    small pieces
Peanut butter or strawberry chia jam
    (see page 67), for topping

Preheat the oven to 350°F (180°C).
Grease a 8 x 4-inch (20 x 10-cm) loaf pan
with coconut oil. Mix the flaxseed and
water in a small bowl and leave to thicken
for 5 minutes.

In a large bowl, combine the flax egg,
bananas, oat milk, almond flour, oats,
cinnamon, cardamom, vanilla powder,
salt, baking powder, and coconut sugar.
Reserve a couple of strawberries, then
fold the rest into the batter. Pour the
batter into the prepared pan. Press the
reserved strawberries on top. Bake for
about 40 minutes and then test with a
toothpick. The bread is ready when no
batter sticks to the toothpick. Take the
bread out of the oven and let it cool completely on a rack before removing it from
the loaf pan. Top with peanut butter or
strawberry chia jam and enjoy.

Vanilla Lingonberry Pancakes

My favorite pancake recipe receives a fresh twist from lingonberries, which go hand in hand with vanilla.

Makes about 6 pancakes

2 ripe bananas
⅔ cup (2 oz/60 g) rolled oats
½ cup (4 fl oz/120 ml) oat milk
½ tsp vanilla powder
1 tbsp coconut sugar
¼ cup (2¾ oz/80 g) lingonberries
    (or 1 tbsp lingonberry powder or ¼ cup
    (1 oz/30 g) cranberries)

TOPPINGS
Berry yogurt
Banana slices
Coconut whipped cream (see page 67)

Place the bananas, oats, oat milk, vanilla powder, and coconut sugar in a blender and blend until smooth. Stir in the lingonberries and leave the batter to thicken for 10 minutes. Warm a medium pan on medium heat. Pour about ¼ cup (1 fl oz/60 ml) of the batter into the pan and make a round pancake. Cook for about 1½ minutes and then flip over. Bake the other side until the pancake is golden brown. Repeat this process with the remaining batter. Serve and enjoy with the toppings of your choice.

Tip! Cranberries are a perfect substitute for lingonberries.

Lilac Cordial

I'm totally crazy about lilac flowers, and this
lilac cordial is my go-to recipe to showcase these vibrant
blooms, which I love to serve with some ice cubes and
sparkling water, white wine, or champagne.

Serves 5

About 4 cups (approx. 10 bunches)
    lilac flowers
1 lemon, sliced
64 fl oz (2 l) of water
⅔ cup (4¾ oz/140 g) erythritol (or xylitol),
    plus more as needed
Juice of 1 lemon

Place the flower bunches on a flat surface, ideally on a garden table so that any bugs can make their way out. Place the lilac flowers in a large jug or glass jar (at least 64 fl oz [2 l] in size, or use many smaller jars) and add the lemon slices. Place the water and erythritol in a medium saucepan. Bring to a boil and stir until the sugar has dissolved. Pour the mixture over the flowers and lemon slices and add the lemon juice on top. Leave the juice to infuse in the refrigerator for 3-4 days. Strain the flowers and lemon from the liquid. Add more erythritol if desired.

Tip! Xylitol and erythritol are natural sweeteners derived from plants. They are both sugar alcohols, but despite their names, they do not contain alcohol. They have fewer calories and carbohydrates than white sugar. I like to use them in recipes where I need to have a light-colored, nonstaining sweetener, like in this cordial, to keep the color pretty and bright.

Lilac Flowers

You can use lilac flowers as edible decorations for cakes, desserts, and ice cream to give a gentle, floral flavor. All lilac varieties are edible, as long as they have not been sprayed with pesticides. Do not consume lilacs bought from flower shops. Harvest lilac branches that have most of the flowers open. An ideal time to pick lilacs is in the early morning or after sunset. Wash the flower bunches under running water. Pick the small florets from the bunches and use them in your recipes.

Pear Quinoa Bowl

This nourishing quinoa-based
warm breakfast bowl is a great alternative
to basic morning oatmeal.

Serves 4

1 cup (8 fl oz/240 ml) water
1 cup (6 oz/170 g) quinoa, rinsed
1 cup (8 fl oz/240 ml) rice milk
  (or oat milk)
2 fresh dates, pitted and sliced
1 medium pear, grated
½ tsp ground cardamom
½ tsp ground ceylon cinnamon

TOPPINGS
Yogurt
Pear slices
Almond butter
Local organic honey (or maple syrup)

In a medium saucepan, bring the water
to a boil. Add the quinoa and rice milk
and simmer on low heat for 10 minutes.
Don't stir too much while cooking so that
the texture doesn't become slimy. Add the
dates, pear, cardamom, and cinnamon.
Slowly simmer for 5 minutes until all the
water has evaporated. Serve with the
toppings of your choice. Enjoy!

Tip! Quinoa is a lovely ingredient for
porridge and oatmeal. It's very nutritious
with essential amino acids, fiber, and
protein, which makes quinoa a great
substitute for oatmeal.

Breakfast Cookies

Bring a bit of summer happiness to your mornings!
These healthy cookies served with your favorite yogurt,
feel-good jam, and berries will be serving you
some sweet and vibrant morning breakfast vibes.

Makes 5 cookies

1¼ cups (4⅓ oz/120 g) rolled oats
¼ cup (1 oz/30 g) quinoa flakes
   (or sunflower seeds)
¼ cup (¾ oz/20 g) sliced almonds
2 tbsp flaxseed
½ tsp ground ceylon cinnamon
½ tsp vanilla powder
¼ cup (2¾ oz/80 g) maple syrup
4 tbsp (2 fl oz/60 ml) melted coconut oil

TOPPINGS
Yogurt
Chia jam (see page 115)
Apricot slices
Raspberries
Pistachios, crushed

Preheat the oven to 350°F (180°C). Line a baking sheet with parchment paper. Place the oats, quinoa flakes, almonds, and flaxseed in a blender or a food processor. Blend until fine. Pour into a medium bowl and add the cinnamon, vanilla powder, maple syrup, and coconut oil. Mix until the dough is smooth. Roll the dough into 5 balls and place them 2 inches (5 cm) apart on the prepared baking sheet. Flatten each cookie with your fingers so that the sides are a bit higher than the middle. Bake for about 15 minutes until the sides are slightly golden. Take out of the oven and let cool completely on a rack. Top with yogurt, chia jam, apricot slices, raspberries, and pistachios. Serve right away.

Chocolate & Black Currant Mousse Parfait

Whether served for breakfast or as a feel-good dessert, chocolate and black currant is a timeless flavor pair and makes this a festive dish for any occasion.

Serves 3

CHOCOLATE MOUSSE

16 ounces (450 g) full-fat coconut milk
   (or 1⅓ cups [11 oz/310 g] coconut cream)
5 tbsp (0.7 oz/20 g) raw cocoa powder
5 tbsp (4 oz/115 g) maple syrup
1 tsp vanilla powder

PARFAIT

½ cup (3 oz/90 g) black currants
1¼ cups (11¼ oz/320 g) natural oat yogurt
   (or coconut yogurt)

TOPPINGS

Grated dark chocolate
Black currants

To make the mousse, place 1⅓ cups (11 fl oz/325 ml) of coconut milk in a small saucepan. Add the cocoa powder, maple syrup, and vanilla powder. Cook on medium heat, stirring constantly, until the mixture boils. Take off the heat. Pour into a glass jar and place in the refrigerator overnight.

To make the parfait, evenly divide the black currants among three small jars. Add the yogurt to each jar on top of the black currants. Add the chocolate mousse to each jar. Sprinkle grated dark chocolate and top with some black currants. Serve and enjoy!

Tip! Decorate the parfaits with lilac and pink corn flowers.

Harvest Blend Juice

This nourishing juice is made from
freshly harvested apples and a few super
healthy sidekicks.

Serves 2

4 apples
2 carrots
6 celery ribs
1-inch (2.5-cm) slice fresh ginger

Place all the ingredients in a blender or
juicer and blend together. Serve as is or
over ice.

Tip! You can vary the amount of apples
in this recipe based on how sweet you
like your juice to be. For my daughter, I
usually add more apples, but when I make
this for myself, I use only 1–2 apples. Try
out what suits your taste buds the best!

Summer Smugglers Blueberry Smoothie

With this delicious blueberry smoothie, you get to enjoy a large amount of greens, even if the taste does not reveal it—a tip for all parents.

Serves 1

1 cup (5 oz/140 g) blueberries
  (fresh or frozen)
1 banana
3 tbsp rolled oats
Handful lettuce
Handful baby spinach
1 cup (8 fl oz/240 ml) oat milk
½ tsp ground ceylon cinnamon
¼ tsp ground cardamom

Place all the ingredients in a blender and blend until smooth. Add more liquid, if needed. Enjoy!

Tip! Try other greens in this smoothie, such as kale, chlorella, or spirulina.

Breakfast Pizza

Pizza for breakfast, anyone?
This fun treat combines familiar morning ingredients
in a new and refreshing way.

Serves 2

2 cups (12 oz/340 g) granola
5 tbsp (4 oz/115 g) peanut butter
4 tbsp (2 fl oz/60 ml) melted coconut oil

TOPPINGS
Coconut yogurt (or oat-based yogurt)
Fresh berries
Figs (or other fruits)

Place the granola, peanut butter, and coconut oil in a large bowl and mix well together. If the peanut butter is super thick, melt it with the coconut oil in a small saucepan. Line a freezer-safe rimmed baking sheet or pizza pan with parchment paper and press the granola mixture into the bottom to create a crust that is ½ inch (12 mm) thick.

Freeze for 1 hour or overnight. Take out of the freezer and gently transfer onto a serving plate. Top with yogurt, berries, figs, or other fruits. Serve while cold.

Tip! This recipe is very versatile, and I always use berries and fruits that are in season. Honestly, almost everything works with this one.

Berry Yogurt Bites

These fun little bites are perfect for both
the breakfast table and snack time with the kids.
Try this recipe with any type of berry you like!

Makes 12 pieces

½ cup (4½ oz/130 g) oat yogurt
⅓ cup (1½ oz/40 g) blueberries
¼ cup (1½ oz/40 g) black currants
⅓ cup (3½ oz/100 g) maple syrup
2–3 tbsp cashew butter (or other
  nut butter)

Pour the yogurt into a medium bowl
and stir in the blueberries and black
currants. Spoon in the maple syrup and
cashew butter. Stir lightly with a spoon
so that it leaves nice white stripes. Spoon
into chocolate trays or ice cube molds
and freeze for couple of hours.

Note! If you are allergic to nuts, replace
the peanut butter with coconut cream.

Flower Sprinkles

I love to collect a variety of edible flowers over the summer months, which I then dry and use as decorations throughout the year.

Collect petals of edible flowers and spread them on a flat tray, kitchen towel, or windowsill. Leave to dry for a day or two. Once the flowers are dry, pour them into a large, sealable glass jar. Use them throughout year on top of the desserts or as a garnish in other dishes, such as salads.

Tip! I like making different kinds of flower sprinkle mixes based on flower colors. For example, in my pink mix I use rose petals and red cornflower; in my yellow mix I use marigold, yellow lilacs, and chamomile; and in my purple mix, I use purple lilacs, cornflower, mallow, and lavender—and in the rainbow mix, everything is mixed together!

Strawberry Basil Parfait

This fragrant summer dessert is a totally unexpected
flavor pairing of strawberry and basil.

Serves 2-3

CHIA PUDDING

1 cup (8 fl oz/240 ml) oat milk
5 tbsp (2 oz/60 g) chia seeds
1 tsp local organic honey (or maple syrup)
1 tsp vanilla extract

SMOOTHIE

1½ cups (13½ oz/380 g) natural oat yogurt
1½ cups (7½ oz/210 g) frozen strawberries,
 thawed but still frosty
½ cup (1¾ oz/50 g) rolled oats
½ cup (½ oz/15 g) fresh basil leaves
Juice of ½ lime
3 tbsp local organic honey
 (or maple syrup)
1 tsp vanilla extract

To make the chia pudding, pour the oat
milk into a jar and stir in the chia seeds,
honey, and vanilla extract. Let thicken
for 10 minutes. Stir again and leave to
thicken in the refrigerator overnight to
get a thick pudding.

To make the smoothie, place all the
ingredients in a blender and blend until
smooth. Taste and adjust ingredients, if
needed. Pour into jars and top with chia
pudding.

Forest Chai Latte

This tea brings the wonderful flavors and scents of the forest to cooler summer mornings or approaching autumn. It's also a perfect drink for a hike or picnic in the forest, when packed in a thermos.

Makes around 12 servings

FOREST CHAI MIXTURE

⅔ cup spruce sprouts (or spruce needles), fresh or dried

1 cup heather flowers, fresh or dried

2 tbsp crushed cinnamon stick

2 tbsp dried minced ginger

2 tbsp cardamom seeds

2 tbsp crushed star anise

2 tsp crushed allspice

FOREST CHAI LATTE

½ cup (4 fl oz/120 ml) water

½ cup (4 fl oz/120 ml) oat milk

½ tsp local organic honey

To make the forest chai mixture, place all the ingredients in a glass jar and mix thoroughly. If you use spruce sprouts, chop them into small pieces with scissors. If you use fresh spruce sprouts, spruce needles, or heather flowers, leave the glass jar lid open for a week or two to allow them to dry. If you use dried needles, store the tea mixture in a closed jar, protected from light, at room temperature and use within a few months.

To make the forest chai latte, combine the water and oat milk in a small saucepan and bring to a near boil. Mix the tea mixture in the jar with a spoon (the lighter ingredients will sink to the bottom), then take a heaping tablespoon of the mixture and place it in a tea strainer. Place the strainer on top of a tea cup, pour the hot water mixture over the tea mixture, and leave to infuse for at least 5 minutes. Sweeten with the honey and enjoy.

Fresh Start Smoothie Bowl

This delicious smoothie sure gets you going in the morning!

Serves 1

1 frozen banana
½ mango
Juice of ½ lemon
Big handful baby spinach
1 tsp grated fresh ginger
½ tsp grated fresh turmeric
Pinch ground black pepper
1 tsp coconut oil
Handful fresh mint
Handful fresh lemon balm

TOPPINGS
Blueberries
Kiwi
Nuts
Raisins

Cut the banana and mango into pieces and place in a blender. Add the remaining ingredients. Blend until smooth. Add water in small portions, if needed, so that the texture remains thick. Pour the smoothie into a bowl and add the toppings. Enjoy!

Tip! Turmeric is one of my favorite ingredients to add to almost everything. It has been used in India for thousands of years as both a spice and medicinal herb for its anti-inflammatory and antioxidant properties. Curcumin, the main active ingredient in turmeric, becomes bioactive and is better absorbed into your body when used with black pepper and some fat.

Whipped Strawberry Apple Porridge

This lovely whipped porridge is easily prepared in a blender for those hectic mornings.

Serves 1

2 cups (16 fl oz/473 ml) rice milk
  (or almond milk)
2 apples, cored and sliced
1½ cups (7½ oz/210 g) strawberries
2 cups (16 fl oz/473 ml) water
1½ cups (8 oz/225 g) rice flour
½ tsp vanilla powder
Sweetener (optional)

TOPPINGS
Rice milk
Apple slices
Berries
Coconut flakes

Place the rice milk in a blender. Add the apple and strawberries. Blend until smooth. If you would like the porridge to be extra fluffy, whip it on a full speed with an electric mixer for 1 minute. Pour the mixture into a saucepan and add the water. Bring to a boil and add the rice flour while whisking continuously. Turn the heat to low and cook the mixture for 10 minutes, stirring occasionally. Stir in the vanilla powder. Take the pan off the heat and let the porridge cool completely. Add sweetener, if desired. Whip until fluffy with an electric mixer. Serve with rice milk, apple slices, berries, and coconut flakes.

Tip! You can substitute rice flour with buckwheat flakes and cook the apple slices and strawberries with the buckwheat flakes, blending the porridge to smooth after it's been cooked.

Summer Heaven Bowl

Unleash your inner food stylist and whip up
this happy and colorful breakfast bowl.

Serves 1-2

VANILLA NICE CREAM

2 frozen overripe bananas, cut into pieces
1 tbsp maple syrup
1 tsp vanilla extract
2-4 tbsp coconut milk (or oat milk),
   if needed

SMOOTHIE

½ cup (2 oz/60 g) raspberries
½ cup (2½ oz/70 g) strawberries
½ cup (4 fl oz/120 ml) almond milk
½ cup (4½ oz/130 g) oat yogurt
½ cup (1¾ oz/50 g) rolled oats
1 tsp maple syrup

TOPPINGS

Granola
Banana slices
Berries
Peanut butter

To make the vanilla nice cream, place
all the ingredients in a blender or food
processor and blend until soft. Add
the coconut milk, if needed, to obtain
a smooth consistency. Spoon the nice
cream into a small serving bowl (or bowls)
so that it fills one side of the bowl.

To make the smoothie, place all the
ingredients in a blender and blend until
smooth. Using a spatula or a big spoon,
add smoothie to the other side of the
bowl. Serve with the toppings of your
choice and enjoy.

Tip! Don't throw overripe bananas away,
as they make the best base for nice
cream! Just cut them into pieces, freeze
in a sealable container, and blend them
until a soft serve ice cream consistency
whenever you're craving some feel-good
ice cream.

Strawberries & Cream Crêpes

A summer classic that can easily
be prepared gluten-free and without dairy.

Makes about 5 crêpes

CRÊPES
1 cup (4 oz/115 g) oat flour
5 tbsp (2 oz/60 g) potato starch
2 tbsp xylitol
Pinch sea salt
1 tsp vanilla extract
1¼ cups (10 fl oz/300 ml) sparkling water
2 tbsp melted coconut oil

COCONUT WHIPPED CREAM
16 ounces (450 g) full-fat coconut milk,
    kept in the refrigerator
2–4 tbsp maple syrup
1 tsp vanilla extract

STRAWBERRY CHIA JAM
1¼ cups (6¼ oz/180 g) strawberries
1 tbsp chia seeds
1 tbsp xylitol (or erythritol or local
    organic honey)

TOPPINGS
Strawberries, sliced
Fresh mint, minced

To make the crêpes, heat a medium nonstick pan over medium heat. Mix the oat flour, potato starch, xylitol, and salt in a medium bowl. Add the vanilla extract, sparkling water, and coconut oil. Stir until smooth. Add a drop of coconut oil onto the pan and pour about ¼ cup (2 fl oz/60 ml) of batter so that you get a thin, round crêpe. Cook until the surface looks dry, flip with a thin spatula, and cook the other side until dry. Repeat this process with the remaining batter.

To make the coconut whipped cream, place the coconut milk in a large bowl. Add the maple syrup and vanilla extract and whip with a mixer until nice and fluffy. If the mixture becomes too liquid, place it in the freezer for about 10 minutes.

To make the strawberry chia jam, chop and mash the strawberries in a small bowl, using a spoon or fork. Add the chia seeds and xylitol. Pour the mixture into a glass jar and leave to thicken in the refrigerator for 10 minutes. Stir and then leave to thicken at least 1 hour. Spread some strawberry chia jam onto the crêpe and top with a couple of dollops of coconut whipped cream. Roll the crêpe and enjoy!

Daytime

Creamy Avocado Pasta

This velvety dish has loads of hidden fresh vegetables and green vitality—in addition to being super easy to make. It's one of my favorite go-to recipes.

Serves 2-3

NETTLE PESTO

4 cups (4 oz/115 g) fresh nettle leaves, rinsed
¼ cup (2 oz/60 g) pine nuts
⅔ cup (3 oz/ 90g) cashew nuts, soaked for 1 hour and then rinsed
⅔ cup (5½ fl oz/160 ml) olive oil
2 tbsp lemon juice
1 clove garlic
½ tsp sea salt

AVOCADO PASTA

1 pound (450 g) pasta of choice
2 avocados, pitted, peeled, and diced
Juice of ½ lemon
1 cup (4 oz/115 g) chopped zucchini
¼ cup (1 oz/30 g) cashews
2 cloves garlic
Big handful fresh basil leaves
Sea salt
Ground black pepper

TOPPINGS

Pine nuts
Basil leaves
Organic Parmesan cheese (or vegan Parmesan cheese)
Chopped avocado (optional)
Edible flowers (optional)

To make the nettle pesto, in a large saucepan boil the nettle leaves with about 40 ounces (1.2 l) water for 3 minutes. Strain the leaves. Save the water for later. Rinse the leaves quickly with cold water and squeeze out the extra liquid. Place the leaves in a blender and add the pine nuts, cashews, olive oil, lemon juice, garlic, and salt. Blend until smooth. If the mixture feels too thick, add some reserved cooking water that you saved. (Use the rest of the water as a hair rinse, see page 159.) Taste and add more salt as needed.

To make the avocado pasta, cook the pasta until tender according to the instructions on the package. Place the avocados, lemon juice, zucchini, cashews, garlic, basil, and 5 tbsp pesto sauce (2 oz/63 g) of nettle pesto in a high-speed blender or a food processor. Season to taste with salt and pepper, then blend until smooth. Pour the sauce on top of the pasta, stir gently, and add the toppings. Enjoy while warm.

Raspberry Leaves

Aromatic red raspberry leaves make lovely ingredients for teas, salads, and stews. They are packed with antioxidants, vitamins A, B, and C, and a number of minerals. Harvest the leaves preferably before the plant blooms and pick them in the morning. Choose vibrant, young, green leaves, rinse them, and pat them dry. You can use them fresh or dried. Raspberry leaves are known as a women's herb and are used to support urinary tract health, menstrual cramps, late pregnancy, and recovery from childbirth. Raspberry leaf also has soothing effects, so try them for relieving tension, soothing the stomach, or as an evening tea.

Spring Comfort Bowl

Sweet potato fries and cinnamon-roasted chickpeas
are the star ingredients in this soothing comfort food dish.

Serves 2

SWEET POTATO FRIES

2 sweet potatoes, peeled and cut
    into sticks
2 tbsp olive oil
Pinch sea salt
Ground black pepper

CINNAMON-ROASTED CHICKPEAS

2 cups (12 oz/340 g) chickpeas
    (cooked or canned)
2 tbsp olive oil
1 tsp ground ceylon cinnamon
Pinch sea salt

DRESSING

¼ cup (2 fl oz/60 ml) full-fat coconut milk
1–2 tbsp almond butter
1 tbsp apple cider vinegar
1 tbsp almond oil (or sesame oil)
1 tbsp soy sauce
2 tbsp lemon juice
1 tsp maple syrup

VEGETABLES

1 bunch asparagus
1 ear sweet corn, sliced
1 cup (1 oz/30 g) baby spinach
1 cup (1 oz/30 g) arugula
1 avocado, pitted, peeled, and sliced
Handful sweet peas

To make the sweet potato fries, preheat
the oven to 400°F (200°C). Line a baking sheet
with parchment paper and add the sweet
potatoes, leaving room between them. Add
the olive oil and season to taste with salt and
pepper, tossing to coat. Bake for 30 minutes.
While they are baking, prepare the chickpeas
so that both can bake at the same time.

To make the cinnamon-roasted chickpeas,
line a baking sheet with parchment paper
and set aside. Dry the chickpeas slightly
with a paper towel and remove most of the
skins. Add the olive oil, cinnamon, and salt
and mix well. Place the chickpeas on the
prepared baking sheet and roast for 30
minutes. Remove from the oven and cool.

To make the dressing, place all ingredients in a small bowl and stir with a spoon
until smooth.

To make the vegetables, prepare a
steamer basket. Add the asparagus and
steam for about 5 minutes, until crisp tender.

Lightly oil a pan and set it over medium
heat. Add the corn and cook for a few minutes until lightly colored.

Divide the baby spinach and arugula
between 2 bowls. Add sweet potato fries,
roasted chickpeas, steamed asparagus,
sweet corn, avocado, and sweet peas. Top
with sunflower sprouts and edible flowers.
Drizzle with dressing and enjoy!

June Sandwiches with No-Tuna Filling

These tasty sandwiches with a plant-based filling are a sure hit if you enjoy classic tuna sandwiches.

Makes 4 sandwiches

10½ ounces (300 g) chickpeas (cooked or canned)

6 tbsp (3 fl oz/90 ml) mayo (or vegan mayo)

1 pickle, chopped

1 small red onion

2 tsp lemon juice

1 tsp maple syrup (or local organic honey)

¼ tsp sea salt

Small handful fresh dill

Ground black pepper

1–2 tbsp Dijon mustard

8 slices toasted bread

TOPPINGS

Sprouts

Avocado, pitted, peeled, and sliced

Fresh dill

Edible flowers, such as dill flowers, oregano flowers, chive blossoms, or violets

Smash the chickpeas in a medium bowl. Leave some whole chickpeas in the mixture. Stir in the mayo, pickles, red onion, lemon juice, maple syrup, salt, dill, and pepper. Add a little bit of mustard, taste, and then add more, if needed. Taste and add salt and pepper as needed. If the mixture feels too thick, add a small amount of water, 1 tablespoon at a time.

To assemble the sandwiches, spread filling onto 1 piece of toast. Then add a generous amount of sprouts. Top with avocado slices and dill. Add some edible flowers on top, add another piece of toast, and use the remaining flowers to decorate the toast. Serve and enjoy!

Chive Blossom Butter

Chive blossoms taste a bit like honey and garlic and are a wonderful addition to many dishes—plus they make everything look extra cute!

Makes about 3½ ounces (100 g)

3½ ounces (100 g) organic unsalted butter (or vegan butter)
10 chive blossoms
3 chives, minced
Pinch sea salt

Soften butter to room temperature. Pick and separate the small chive blossoms from their florets and pour them into a bowl. Make sure no bugs get in. Add the chives, softened butter, and salt. Mix well. Scrape the butter mixture into decorative ice cube molds (or a small jar or bowl). Cool the butter in the refrigerator until solid. Serve the butter cubes with bread. If cooled in a jar or bowl, scrape small butter balls with a small ice-cream scoop and serve on a plate.

Dandelion Petal Bread Rolls

As a child, I used to make bread rolls out of sand and dandelion petals in a sandbox in my grandmother's yard. But as an adult, I found dandelion petals work really well in real bread rolls, too. Do try it!

Makes 6 rolls

½ cup (1¾ oz/50 g) coconut flour
⅔ cup (3½ oz/100 g) potato starch
½ tsp sea salt
1 tsp baking powder
⅔ cup dandelion petals, plus more
  for garnish
½ cup (4 fl oz/120 ml) olive oil
¼ cup (2 fl oz/60 ml) water
2 large organic eggs (or 2 tbsp flaxseed
  + 5 tbsp [21½ fl oz/75 ml] water)

Preheat the oven to 350°F (180°C) and line a baking sheet with parchment paper. In a large bowl, mix together the coconut flour, potato starch, salt, baking powder, and dandelion petals. Add the olive oil and water. Stir. In another bowl, lightly beat the eggs, then add them to the batter, stirring to combine. (Or mix the flaxseed and water in a small bowl and leave to thicken for 5 minutes, then add to the batter.) Leave dough to thicken for 5 minutes. If the dough is too loose, add 1 tablespoon of coconut flour at a time to thicken. If the dough is too dry and crumbly, add a little bit of water to loosen. Shape the dough into small rolls about 3 inches (7.5 cm) wide, then transfer to the prepared baking sheet. Garnish with dandelion petals. Bake the rolls for about 30 minutes until slightly golden.

8-Veggie Garden Pasta

Here is one of our family's everyday favorites. This wonderfully tasty pasta sauce hides an insane amount of vegetables, which kids will love—and will not even notice the healthy ingredients!

Serves 3

2 tbsp olive oil
1 white onion, diced
2 cloves garlic
1 celery rib, diced
2 carrots, grated
1 zucchini, diced
1 yellow bell pepper, diced
½ tsp sea salt
25 ounces (710 g) tomato purée
½ cup (5 oz/140 g) canned chickpeas
Small bunch fresh oregano
Small bunch fresh basil
Ground black pepper
1 pound (450 g) gluten-free pasta
  of choice

TOPPING
Parmesan (or nutritional yeast)

Warm the olive oil in a medium pan over low heat. Add the onion and cook, stirring, for about 3 minutes until softened. Add the garlic and cook for about 30 seconds, until fragrant. Increase the heat to medium and add the celery and carrots. Cook for 5 minutes. Add the zucchini, bell pepper, and salt and cook for about 5 minutes. Finally, add the tomato purée, chickpeas, oregano, basil, and pepper. Cook for 10–15 minutes until the vegetables have softened. While vegetables are cooking, cook the pasta until tender according to the instructions on the package. Transfer the vegetables to a blender and blend into a smooth sauce. Taste and add salt and pepper as needed. Serve sauce with pasta. Add Parmesan on top and enjoy!

Floral Ice Cubes

No other drink makes you as happy as one served with flower ice cubes. I use large ice-cube molds so that the cubes stay cold for a longer time.

Edible flowers
Water
Lemon juice

Place the flowers into ice-cube molds. Cut the petals into small shreds if needed. Fill the molds with water. If you would like clear ice cubes, use cold water. If, on the other hand, you would like the petals to dispense and color the ice cubes, use warm water. If necessary, press the petals under water. Squeeze a few drops of lemon juice into the water. Place the molds in the freezer until the ice cubes are completely frozen.

Tip! Additional vibrant flowers, such as mallow, lilac, and carnations, or fresh herbs, such as thyme, rosemary, oregano, sage, and basil, also work really well.

Edible Flowers

Try different edible flowers to decorate your dishes, such as roses, violets, lilacs, cornflower, clover, fireweed, strawberry, blue tansy, lingonberry, blueberry, verbena, perennial phlox, carnations, and mallow flowers. The best time to pick flowers is early morning or late afternoon. After picking, gently wash away any dirt with cold water. Place on paper towels and store in the refrigerator and use within a few days. You can also dry them by spreading the flowers on a flat surface, such as a baking sheet, in a dry place. In a sunny place it takes only one day until they are fully dry. Store the flowers in a sealed jar in a dark spot, as the sun will fade the colors. Use within a year. Edible flowers are a perfect addition to all kinds of desserts, or they can be tossed into salads, ice cubes, and drinks, or used on top of toast. Use only flowers you know are clean and are grown without pesticides. Do not use flowers from commercial florists or those picked from the roadside or in public parks.

Summer Grazing Board

For an easy, affordable, and pretty way to
serve food to summer guests, try two different kinds of
grazing boards for the most lavish-looking spreads!

Carrot sticks, snap peas, radishes,
asparagus, grapes, apple slices, pear
slices, dates, figs, olives, nuts, cheeses,
hummus, dips, crackers, breadsticks,
edible flowers.

SWEET GRAZING BOARD
Strawberries, blueberries, cake slices,
marshmallows, toffee, chocolate, dried
mango, dried apple, popcorn, meringues,
oatmeal cookies, macarones, edible
flowers.

Spread a white tablecloth on the table
and then place parchment paper on top.
Tightly arrange the food items on top of
the parchment paper so that they form
small clusters and the parchment paper
isn't visible. Spoon dips and hummus
directly onto the parchment paper or
small plates. Place small spoons for the
dips and knives for the cheeses. Garnish
with plenty of edible flowers. Arrange
plates, napkins, and cocktail sticks at the
end of the table.

Tip! Place chilled trays under the tablecloth to keep food cold and fresh.

Strawberry Basil Salad

This easy salad has become our family's summer favorite. It is a perfect accompaniment when we are grilling.

Serves 2

2 cups (2 oz/60 g) baby spinach
Big bunch fresh basil
1¼ cups (6¼ oz/180 g) fresh strawberries, sliced

LEMON DRESSING
4 tbsp olive oil
1 tbsp balsamic vinegar
1 tbsp lemon juice
½ tsp lemon zest
Pinch sea salt
Ground black pepper

TOPPING
3½ ounces (100 g) organic feta (or vegan cheese)

Combine the spinach, basil, and strawberries in a large salad bowl. In a small bowl, whisk together the olive oil, balsamic vinegar, lemon juice, lemon zest, salt, and pepper. Taste and adjust the salt and pepper as needed. Pour the dressing over the salad and mix lightly. Crumble the feta on top, then serve and enjoy!

Tip! This salad is perfect when served with bread and grilled veggies.

Sunshine Tofu Poke Bowl

This nourishing and filling delicacy bowl will certainly put you in a good mood.

Serves 2

30 ounces (850 g) canned chickpeas, drained, patted dry, and skins mostly removed

2 tbsp olive oil

½ tsp sea salt

10½ ounces (300 g) firm tofu

2 tbsp soy sauce

2 tbsp sriracha

2 tsp garlic powder

2 cups (14 oz/404 g)cooked rice (or quinoa)

1 avocado, peeled, pitted, cubed

½ mango, cubed

2 tbsp pickled onion

2 tbsp sauerkraut

4 radishes, sliced

¼ cucumber, diced

4 tbsp (1¼ oz/35 g) hemp seeds

Fresh mint

Juice of 1 lime

SAUCE

4 tbsp (2½ oz/70 g) light tahini

3 tbsp rice milk (or oat milk)

Juice of ½ lemon

1 tsp local organic honey (or maple syrup)

1 tsp sriracha

1 clove garlic, minced

½ tsp Dijon mustard

Pinch sea salt

Preheat the oven to 400°F (200°C). Line 2 baking sheets with parchment papers. Prepare the chickpeas and tofu as follows and roast them at the same time. Boil the rice (or quinoa) while the chickpeas and quinoa are roasting.

Place the chickpeas on 1 baking sheet. Add the oil and salt, tossing to coat.

Cut the tofu into small cubes and pour into a bowl. Add the soy sauce, sriracha, and garlic powder. Mix well. Transfer to the second baking sheet. Place both baking sheets in the oven and roast for about 30 minutes until the chickpeas are crisp and the tofu cubes are golden yellow and crispy. Be sure to stir the chickpeas halfway through.

To make the sauce, whisk together all the ingredients in a small bowl.

To prepare one bowl, add about 1 cup of cooked rice to bottom of serving bowl. Top with about ¼ cup of tofu and ¼ cup of chickpeas. Add half of avocado and mango and half of pickled onion, sauerkraut, sliced radishes, and cucumber. Sprinkle with hemp seeds. Top with fresh mint and squeeze of lime juice. Top with sauce.

Infused Waters

Not only are flavored waters total life savers on warm summer days, they are also tasty and beautiful drinks for guests. Try these flavors and find your own favorite!

Serves 4

34 fl oz (1 l) water (still or sparkling)
Floral Ice Cubes (see page 84)

COTTAGE SPA DRINK
2 lemon slices
5 cucumber slices
5 fresh basil leaves

STRAWBERRY FLOWER DRINK
½ cup (2½ oz/70 g) strawberries, sliced
3 lemon slices
2 fresh lavender sprigs (or handful of
   wild rose petals)

GODDESS REFRESHMENT
1 peach or nectarine, sliced
½ orange, sliced
5 fresh basil leaves

GRAPEFRUIT COOLER
1 grapefruit, sliced
Small handful cilantro

SUMMER GULP
1 cup (8 oz/225 g) cubed watermelon
Pulp of 1 passion fruit
1 lime, sliced
Small handful fresh mint

Mix all the ingredients of choice except the ice cubes in a large jug or bottle. Transfer the drink to the refrigerator to infuse overnight or for 12 hours. Add the ice cubes before serving. After finishing the water, refill the same bottle or jug with water or mineral water if the fruits and berries are still good. Store in the refrigerator.

Tip! Always use fresh ingredients for the best flavor. Citrus rinds can sometimes give a bitter flavor, so cut the rinds off if you would like a sweeter flavor.

July Potato Salad

Potato salad is a must-have for our barbecue evenings as well as a delicious dish to enjoy for lunch.

Serves 2

CHICKPEA MASH

10½ ounces (300 g) chickpeas (cooked or canned)

4 tbsp (2 fl oz/60 ml) plant-based mayo (or tahini)

3 tbsp capers

3 tbsp minced chives

2 tbsp yellow mustard

2 tsp lemon juice

1 tsp maple syrup (or raw organic honey)

¼ tsp sea salt

Small handful fresh dill

Ground black pepper

FOR THE SALAD

5 potatoes, boiled and cut into chunks

5 kale leaves

TOPPINGS

Clover flowers

Chive blossoms

Minced chives

Thyme flowers

In a medium bowl, smash the chickpeas with a fork. Leave some whole chickpeas in the mixture. Add the mayo, capers, chives, mustard, lemon juice, maple syrup, salt, and dill. Taste and add salt and pepper as needed. I recommend adding a little of the mustard first and tasting.

Add the potatoes and stir to combine. Serve with the kale, and top with flowers and herbs.

Tip! Salads are a great place to add a variety of herbs and edible flowers. They make everything look stunning and are a great source for a wide variety of vitamins, minerals, and essential oils.

Summer Tacos

These tacos include vegan taco meat, which is light, filling, and wonderfully nourishing. Give it a try with taco shells or crispy lettuce leaves.

Serves 3

VEGAN TACO MEAT

1¼ cups (5 oz/140 g) chopped walnuts

½ cup (1¾ oz/50 g) oil-packed sun-dried tomatoes, drained

5½ cups (11 oz/310 g) cauliflower florets, cut into tiny pieces (about 1 medium cauliflower)

½ red onion, minced

1 tsp cumin

½ tsp chili powder

½ tsp garlic powder

½ tsp sea salt

Juice of 1 lime

FOR THE SHELLS

Crispy lettuce (like romaine lettuce)

Taco shells

TOPPINGS

Avocado, pitted, peeled, and diced

Tomato, diced

Salsa

Fresh cilantro

Any other fillings of choice

Preheat the oven to 350°F (180°C) and line a baking sheet with a parchment paper. Place the walnuts into a food processor or blender and blend into crumbs. Squeeze excess oil from the sun-dried tomatoes and add them to the food processor. Add the cauliflower, onion, cumin, chili powder, garlic powder, salt, and lime juice. Chop into a smooth consistency. Scrape the mixture onto the baking sheet and spread evenly. Bake the mixture for 40–45 minutes, stirring once or twice. Take out of the oven. Place the filling in the lettuce or taco shells, add the toppings of your choice, and serve.

Tip! If you want make the healthiest taco shells, skip fried flour tortillas and try nonfried corn tortillas, lettuce wraps, purple cabbage, or even bell pepper halves!

Pear Cabbage Salad

I always come back to this simple salad over and over again. The crispy cabbage, juicy pear, and fresh mint is a lovely winning combo.

Serves 2

2 cups (6 oz/170 g) chopped green
   cabbage
2 sweet pears
5 boiled potatoes
Handful fresh mint leaves
1 tbsp minced chives
Grilled zucchini
Halloumi (or vegan cheese cubes)

DRESSING
3 tbsp olive oil
1 tbsp apple cider vinegar
Juice of ½ lemon
Pinch sea salt
Ground black pepper

TOPPINGS
Chive blossoms
Fresh herbs of choice
Edible flowers of choice

Place the cabbage in a large bowl. Cut the pears and potatoes into small pieces and add to bowl. Add the mint. In a small bowl, whisk together the olive oil, vinegar, and lemon juice. Taste and add salt and pepper as needed. Pour the dressing over the salad ingredients. Mix with clean hands to season the salad evenly. Transfer to the refrigerator to marinate for 10 minutes. Add the zucchini and halloumi. If you serve the salad the next day, add the pear pieces just before serving so they don't darken. Add the toppings of your choice and serve.

Clover Ice Tea

This cute drink is mildly sweet and a great refreshment.

Serves 2

½ cup fresh clover flowers
2 cups (16 fl oz/475 ml) water

FOR SERVING
Lemon slices
1 tsp local organic honey

Spread the clover flowers on a flat surface so that any bugs can find their way out. Rinse the flowers and place them in a large glass jar. Bring the water to a boil and pour into the jar over the flowers. Let it cool and transfer to the refrigerator to infuse overnight. Strain to remove flowers the next day. Serve and enjoy with ice cubes, lemon slices, and the honey. Store in a resealable jar in the refrigerator and use within a couple of days.

Clover

Both the vitamin-rich leaves and flowers of all common clover varieties, such as white clover and red clover, are edible. Harvested during early summer, they are wonderful additions to salads, sandwiches, and other dishes. Flowers are rich in flavonoids, which makes them great in tinctures, wine, juice, and syrup. Leaves and flowers can also be dried and used in herbal drinks or even skin-care recipes (see pages 149–162). For example, flower water made from dried clover flowers is great as a toner and is perfect for dry and aging skin.

To harvest clover, pick the flowers and leaves in the early morning or late afternoon. Rinse them in cold water and place on a paper towel. Store in the refrigerator and use within a few days. Clover, especially red clover, has been used as herbal medicine to remove mucus, prevent inflammation, help the urinary tract, and lower cholesterol.

Carrot Fries & Curry Dip

These bright and cheery fries, paired with
a delicious curry dip, are perfect for
get-togethers and movie nights!

Serves 2

17 ounces (480 g) carrots
1 tbsp potato starch
1 tbsp olive oil
½ tsp sea salt
Ground black pepper
½ cup (2 oz/60 g) grated Parmesan
   (or 2 tbsp nutritional yeast)
1 bunch fresh cilantro, for garnish

CURRY DIP
½ cup (4½ oz/130 g) natural Greek yogurt
   (or oat fraiche)
¼ cup (2 fl oz/60 ml) mayo (or vegan mayo)
1 tbsp local organic honey
Juice of 1 lime
1–2 tsp curry powder
Pinch sea salt
Ground black pepper

TOPPING
Cilantro

Preheat the oven to 425°F (220°C) and line a baking sheet with parchment paper. Peel the carrots and cut to french fry–size sticks. Transfer to a large bowl and add the potato starch, olive oil, salt, pepper, and Parmesan. (If using nutritional yeast, add after baking.) Mix well. Transfer the seasoned carrots to the prepared baking sheet and spread out evenly. Bake for 15–20 minutes, stirring halfway through the cooking time, until the carrots are slightly tender but still hold their shape.

   Meanwhile, in a small bowl, make the curry dip by whisking together the yogurt, mayo, honey, lime juice, and curry powder. Taste and add salt and pepper as needed. When the carrots are done, garnish with the cilantro and serve with the dip.

Baked Nettle Chips

Stinging nettle, commonly found in backyards,
is transformed into a wonderfully crunchy snack!

Serves 2

2 cups (2 oz/60 g) young stinging
   nettle leaves
2 tbsp olive oil
1 tsp sea salt
½ tsp garlic powder

Preheat the oven to 300°F (150°C). Line
a baking sheet with parchment paper.
Rinse and dry the stinging nettle leaves.
Place the leaves in a large bowl and add
the olive oil, salt, and garlic powder. Mix
so that all the leaves are seasoned. Place
the leaves on the baking sheet and spread
evenly. Bake for 5-7 minutes, until the
leaves are dry and dark.

Tip! If you want to add a cheesy flavor
to your chips, sprinkle some nutritional
yeast on top of them after baking.

Stinging Nettle

Young stinging nettle shoots (also called nettle) are massive nutrient bombs. Cut the shoots 4–6 inches (10–15 cm) long using protective gloves. Their burning sensation disappears after the leaves are dried completely, boiled in water, or thoroughly pureed. New shoots will appear later in the summer after being cut. Use dried or parboiled nettle in soups, stews, breads, and pancakes. Dried nettle leaves make a great herbal tea. You can also blend dried nettle leaves into a powder and add 1 teaspoon (or 1 tablespoon) a day to your smoothies, oatmeal, or yogurt. It is a brilliant supplement for hair and nail growth! I also collect nettle seeds in the fall, which I dry and store in a glass jar and then sprinkle over oatmeal and porridge during the winter. Do not collect or use nettle that grows near compost, livestock farms, or in areas fertilized with nitrogen.

Sweet

Raw PB & Chia Jam Ice Pops

Too delish to miss! These treats are absolutely at their best when enjoyed right after you've made them.

Makes about 6 ice pops

NICE CREAM

1 cup (4 oz/115 g) cashews, soaked for
   5 hours and rinsed
½ cup (4 fl oz/120 ml) full-fat coconut milk
½ cup (4½ oz/130 g) natural coconut
   yogurt
1 tsp lemon juice
1 drop liquid stevia
1 tsp xylitol
1 tsp vanilla extract

CHIA JAM

⅔ cup (2½ oz/70 g) raspberries
3 tbsp chia seeds
1 tbsp local organic honey

PEANUT BUTTER FILLING

½ cup (5 oz/140 g) peanut butter

COATING

3½ ounces (100 g) dark chocolate, melted
Peanut butter
Coconut flakes

To make the nice cream, put all the ingredients into a blender and blend until super smooth. Add a bit more coconut milk or yogurt, if needed, but keep as thick as possible. Taste and add more sweetener as needed. Pour the nice cream mixture into molds and freeze for 2 hours or until solid.

To prepare the chia jam, mash the raspberries and add the chia seeds. Add the honey, if needed. Leave to thicken for 2 hours.

Take the ice pops from the freezer and remove the molds. Spread about 1–2 tbsp of peanut butter on top of each ice pop. Then spread on the chia jam. Place in the freezer for 30 minutes.

Dip the ice pops into the melted chocolate. Top with peanut butter swirls or coconut flakes. Place back into the freezer for 30 minutes, until solid. If you store the ice pops in the freezer for longer, let them thaw for 15–20 minutes before serving.

Rhubarb & Rose Crumble

I've prepared this crumble probably a hundred times,
usually on the grill. Our family never seems to get tired
of it, especially when served with vanilla ice cream.

Serves 3-4

2 cups (225 g/8 oz) thinly sliced rhubarb
Big handful wild rose petals
4 tbsp (3 oz/90 g) maple syrup

CRUMBLE TOPPING
2 cups (7 oz/200 g) rolled oats
1½ tsp ground ceylon cinnamon
1 tsp ground cardamom
3 tbsp maple syrup (or coconut sugar)
3 tbsp peanut butter
4 tbsp (2 oz/60 g) organic unsalted butter
    (or ½ cup [4 fl oz/120 ml] melted
    coconut oil)

TOPPINGS
Vanilla ice cream
Wild rose petals

Preheat the oven to 400°F (200°C).
Place the rhubarb and rose petals into
a deep oven-safe dish. Drizzle with the
maple syrup and stir. Prepare the crumble topping by mixing all the ingredients
together with your hands in a medium
bowl. Taste and add more maple syrup
as needed. Spread the topping on top
of the rhubarb mixture. Grill or bake for
15–20 minutes until the rhubarb is soft
and the crumble is golden. Enjoy with the
toppings of your choice

Roses

Wild roses are definitely my favorite ingredients in the summertime. All rose petals are edible. Dark-colored roses have a stronger taste. Try them in desserts, jams, juices, smoothies, or as edible decorations. They are also great for the skin. Collect rose petals in the morning, after the dew has evaporated and when they are the most fragrant. The strongest flavor is found in petals that have just bloomed, but I also like using mature petals that are beginning to fall off (it feels like a gentler way to harvest them). Only eat roses grown outdoors that have not been sprayed with pesticides. Roses purchased from a florist should not be eaten.

Chocolate-Covered Summer Kisses

Nothing is more perfect to round off a summer meal than peanut butter cookies, whipped cream, chocolate, and strawberries!

Makes 12 bonbons

PEANUT BUTTER COOKIES

1 cup (3½ oz/100 g) almond flour
¼ cup (1¾ oz/50 g) coconut sugar
1 tsp baking soda
½ tsp vanilla powder
½ cup (5 oz/140 g) peanut butter
1 tbsp melted coconut oil
Pinch sea salt

ASSEMBLY

Coconut whipped cream (see page 67)
12 big strawberries
Cacao (or dark chocolate), melted

To make the cookies, preheat the oven to 350°F (180°C) and line a baking sheet with parchment paper. In a large bowl, combine all the ingredients and mix well. Divide the dough into 12 small balls. Flatten the balls with your fingers to create round shapes and place on the prepared baking sheet. Bake for 10 minutes until golden. Let cool completely. The cookies should be really soft but will harden in about 30 minutes.

To assemble, place the whipped cream in a piping bag. Place 1 strawberry on top of each peanut butter cookie. Frost the cookies and strawberries with the cream so that it covers the strawberry, creating a bonbon. Place the bonbons in the refrigerator for at least 1 hour for the frosting to harden. Dip the whipped cream top into the melted chocolate. Pop back into the refrigerator to harden. Serve and enjoy!

Grilled Cinnamon Peaches

Are guests coming and you need to whip up something to serve? Don't stress. These grilled cinnamon peaches come to the rescue and will be ready in 15 minutes.

Serves 2-4

4 peaches, pitted and sliced
3 tbsp coconut sugar
1 tsp ground ceylon cinnamon

TOPPINGS
Peanut butter
Rolled oats
Local organic honey (or maple syrup)
Vanilla ice cream (or natural yogurt)

Heat a grill to medium. Place the peaches, with their sliced side facing down, onto the grill and cook for about 5 minutes or until the peaches begin to soften. Flip the peaches and sprinkle with the coconut sugar and cinnamon. Grill for another 5 minutes until the peaches are soft and well cooked. Take them off the grill and place on serving dishes with the sliced side up. Add a teaspoon of peanut butter inside of each slice. Sprinkle with oats and add a small drop of honey on top. Serve warm with vanilla ice cream.

Tip! Flower petals simply make every dessert more pretty and a bit more magical. Impress your guests and sprinkle on some rose petals, lilac flowers, or other edible flowers of your liking. Little things can make a big impact.

Blueberry Dream Cake

This recipe made history went it went viral
on Instagram and was the cover photo
for *Thrive* magazine.

Serves 8-12

CRUST

½ cup (2 oz/60 g) pecans

½ cup (2½ oz/70 g) almonds

7 fresh dates, pitted

½ tsp ground cardamom

Pinch sea salt

FILLING

2 cups (8 oz/225 g) cashews, soaked for
    30 minutes and rinsed

½ ripe banana

½ cup (4 fl oz/120 ml) mild-flavored
    melted coconut oil

6 tbsp (4½ oz/130 g) local organic honey
    (or maple syrup)

⅓ cup (6 fl oz/80 ml) oat milk

2 tbsp full-fat coconut milk

Juice of 1 lemon

1 tsp vanilla extract

½ cup (2½ oz/70 g) blueberries

TOPPINGS

Blueberries

Fresh thyme

To make the crust, cover the bottom of a 7-inch (18-cm) springform pan with parchment paper. Place all the crust ingredients in a food processor or a blender and blend until the dough is able to be molded. Transfer the crust mixture to the prepared pan and firmly press it into the bottom.

Prepare the filling by placing all the filling ingredients except the blueberries in a food processor or blender and blend until smooth. Add some oat milk, if needed, to get a smooth texture, but keep it as thick as possible. Pour about a third of the mixture into the pan and smooth the surface. Add the blueberries into the food processor and blend with the remaining mixture. Taste and adjust the flavor as needed. Spoon the filling into the pan and gently even the surface with a spoon. Top with blueberries. Place the pan in the freezer for about 2–3 hours or until the cake is solid. Remove the cake from the pan and place it on a serving dish. Garnish with blueberries and fresh thyme, serve, and enjoy. Store in the refrigerator.

Cacao Banana Pops

Chocolate-covered frozen bananas are
a well-known treat among health foodies.
Be sure to try this version with choco-yogurt coating!

Makes 8 pops

4 ripe bananas
1 cup (9 oz/250 g) thick coconut yogurt
   (or oat yogurt)
4 tbsp (½ oz/15 g) raw cacao powder
2 tbsp maple syrup
½ tsp vanilla powder

TOPPINGS
Grated chocolate
Coconut flakes
Edible flowers

Peel the bananas and half them. Pour the yogurt into a small bowl and stir in the cacao powder, maple syrup, and vanilla powder. Taste and add more maple syrup as needed. Place a wooden stick in each banana and dip the bananas into the yogurt mixture so that they get a thick coating. Sprinkle with the toppings of your choice. Freeze for about 2 hours or until frozen. Enjoy!

Tip! For an extra chocolate layer, dip the banana pops in melted chocolate.

3-Ingredient Brownies

These are probably the easiest brownies in the world.
This mouthwatering delicacy is a lovely treat
to be enjoyed on a warm summer evening
with vanilla ice cream.

Makes 9 brownies

3 overripe bananas, chopped
½ cup (6½ oz/185 g) almond butter
¼ cup cacao powder

TOPPING
Vanilla ice cream

Preheat the oven to 350°F (180°C).
Grease a 6-inch (15-cm) square cake pan
or line with parchment paper. Place the
bananas and almond butter in a blender.
If the almond butter is hard and thick, add
it first to a small saucepan with 2 tablespoons of coconut oil and melt, stirring
over low heat. Then pour the mixture into
the blender. Finally, add the cacao powder
and mix into a smooth dough. Pour the
batter into the prepared pan and bake for
20–25 minutes. Take the brownies out of
the oven and cool completely, preferably
overnight in the refrigerator. Cut the
brownies into squares and serve with
vanilla ice cream.

Raspberry Fruit Leather

Juicy feel-good candy at its best.

About 7 pieces

2 cups (8 oz/225 g) raspberries
(fresh or frozen)
1 tbsp local organic honey
1 tsp vanilla extract

Preheat the oven to 140°F (60°C). Line a baking sheet with parchment paper. Measure the raspberries, honey, and vanilla extract into a blender and blend until smooth. If you're using frozen raspberries, thaw them first. Pour the purée onto the prepared baking sheet and spread into a ⅛–¼ inch (3mm–6mm) thick layer. Bake for 5 hours until the surface feels dry, but a bit sticky, and the fruit leather peels away easily from the parchment paper. Take out of the oven and let cool overnight. Cut into strips and roll up. Store in an airtight container in the refrigerator and use within a few weeks.

Strawberry & Basil Ice Pops

Easy and refreshing! Strawberry and basil ice pops will cheer you up on a hot summer day. To make an adult version, add 4 tablespoons of vodka.

About 6 ice pops

6 cups (30 oz/850 g) strawberries, stemmed
Juice of 1 lemon
½ cup (½ oz/15 g) fresh basil
5 tbsp (4 oz/115 g) local organic honey (or maple syrup)

Place all ingredients in a blender and blend until smooth. Pour the mixture into ice pop molds and insert ice pop sticks. Freeze for about 4 hours or until completely frozen. Remove from the molds by placing the molds under running warm water for 10 seconds. Enjoy!

Tip! Fresh berries and herbs are a match made in summer heaven. Try substituting strawberries and basil with blueberries and mint or raspberries and thyme. Cranberry and rosemary is a lovely combo, too!

Pear & Raspberry Dream Cake

I call my raw cakes "dream cakes" because they are so dreamy, tasty, and soft. This version showcases a harmonious couple: pear and raspberry.

Serves 6-8

CRUST
½ cup (2½ oz/70 g) almonds
⅓ cup (1 oz/30 g) rolled oats
8 fresh dates, pitted
Pinch sea salt
½ tsp ground cardamom

FILLING
½ cup (4½ oz/130 g) natural oat yogurt
   (or coconut yogurt)
½ cup (2 oz/60 g) cashew nuts, soaked
   for 1 hour and rinsed
1 pear, cored and sliced
1 tsp vanilla powder
2 tbsp local organic honey
⅓ cup (6 fl oz/80 ml) mild-flavored melted
   coconut oil
½ cup (2 oz/60 g) raspberries

TOPPINGS
Pear slices
Raspberries

To make the crust, place the almonds and oats in a blender and blend to a fine texture. Add the dates, salt, and cardamon and blend until the dough is moldable. Line the bottom of a 7-inch (18-cm) cake pan with parchment paper. Transfer the dough to the prepared pan and firmly press it into the bottom.

To make the filling, combine the yogurt, cashews, pear, vanilla powder, honey, and coconut oil to a blender and blend until smooth to create a white mixture. Pour half of the mixture on top of the crust. Add the raspberries to the blender with the remaining mixture and blend. Pour the pink mixture on top of the white mixture. Place the pan in the freezer for 2–3 hours, or until solid. Let thaw for 30 minutes before serving. Decorate with pear slices and raspberries.

Rose Lassi

Yogurt-based lassis are my daughter's favorites.
I usually season them with either mango or strawberries.
But in this recipe, I slipped in a little flower power!

Serves 2

1½ cups (13½ oz/380 g) natural oat yogurt
½ cup (4 fl oz/120 ml) oat milk
½ cup (2½ oz/70 g) strawberries (fresh
 or frozen)
½ cup (approx. 20 petals) wild rose petals
2 tbsp xylitol (or erythritol)
2 tbsp local organic honey
½ tsp ground cardamom
2 ice cubes

Measure all ingredients in a blender and blend until smooth. Serve cold and enjoy.

Tip! Lassis are a traditional and very popular beverage in Indian cuisine that are yogurt based and usually include spices and fruits. You can use Greek yogurt or any natural yogurt as the base. Lassis can be sweet, savory, or spicy. The most popular lassi is mango, which you can make by substituting the strawberries and rose petals with ½ cup (3 oz/90 g) chopped mango in this recipe.

Blueberry Lilac Nice Cream

Blueberries and lilac flowers are one of my signature combos in desserts. Their flavors and shades work beautifully together.

Serves 1-2

2 frozen ripe bananas, cut into pieces
2 tbsp full-fat coconut milk
¼ cup (1¼ oz/35 g) blueberries
About ¼ cup (approx. 1 bunch) lilac flowers
1 tsp vanilla extract

TOPPINGS
Lilac flowers
2 tbsp local organic honey (or
    maple syrup)

Combine all the ingredients in a blender or food processor and blend into a smooth, soft serve ice cream consistency. If your blender is small, you can prepare the ice cream in smaller batches. Enjoy as it is, or freeze for 1 hour to make the ice cream more solid. Serve with the toppings of your choice.

Sweet Love Cupcakes

If you would like to surprise someone with a super cute treat, prepare these!

Makes about 8 cupcakes

CUPCAKES

1 cup (4 oz/115 g) organic gluten-free
   flour blend
½ cup (1¾ oz/50 g) almond flour
1 tsp baking powder
1 tsp baking soda
Pinch sea salt
½ cup (3½ oz/100 g) coconut sugar
¼ cup (2 fl oz/60 ml) melted coconut oil
¼ cup (2 fl oz/60 ml) melted peanut butter
1 cup (8 fl oz/240 ml) oat milk (or other
   vegan milk)
1 tsp apple cider vinegar
1 tsp vanilla extract

COCONUT FROSTING

14 ounces (400 g) full-fat coconut
   milk, cold
2–4 tbsp maple syrup
1 tsp vanilla extract
1 tsp pink pittaya powder (or beet powder)
1 tsp blueberry powder
8 fresh raspberries (or peanut butter)

Preheat the oven to 350°F (180°C). Cover a muffin pan with muffin liners or use silicon molds. In a medium bowl, combine the flour blend, almond flour, baking powder, baking soda, salt, and coconut sugar. Melt the coconut oil and peanut butter in bain-marie until they liquidify. Stir in the oat milk, vinegar, and vanilla extract. Add to the flour mixture, then mix to combine. Pour the batter into the prepared pan and cook for 15–18 minutes. Remove from the oven and let cool.

To make the frosting, open the coconut milk cans and scoop out the white thick paste into a bowl. Add maple syrup, vanilla extract, pittaya powder and blueberry powder. Whip with a mixer until fluffy. If the mixture becomes runny, place it in the refrigerator to thicken. When the muffins are completely cooled, place the frosting in a piping bag or cut a small hole in the corner of a small plastic bag to use for piping. Place 1 raspberry (or 1 teaspoon of peanut butter) on top of each muffin. Frost the muffins and make sure the frosting covers the raspberry. Store in the refrigerator until served.

Watermelon Ice Cream

This fresh and easy recipe screams
summer—and its color is beautiful!

Serves 2-3

2 cups (16 oz/450 g) frozen cubed
  watermelon
14 ounces (400 g) full-fat coconut milk
5 tbsp (4 oz/115 g) maple syrup
½ tsp vanilla powder

Measure all the ingredients in a blender
or a food processor and blend until
smooth. Pour the mixture into a bread
pan and put in the freezer for about
1 hour. Take out of the freezer, scoop out
ice cream balls, and enjoy.

If the ice cream is stored in the freezer
for a longer time, let it thaw at room temperature, cut into small pieces, and puree
in a blender or food processor until soft.

Tip! You can also prepare soft serve ice
cream using ice cube molds. Just pour
the ice cream mixture into the molds
and freeze until solid. Let them thaw just
a bit before popping out. Place the ice
cubes in a food processor or high-speed
blender. Add a couple of tablespoons of
a plant-based milk, then blend until soft
and creamy.

Passion Watermelon Salad

Wake up with this fresh summer fruit salad,
which we often eat for breakfast in our house.

Serves 2-3

1¼ cups (10 oz/285 g) cubed watermelon
1¼ cups (7 oz/200 g) sliced strawberries
2 passion fruits
Juice of 1 lime

DRESSING
½ cup (4½ oz/130 g) natural yogurt
2 tbsp maple syrup (or local
 organic honey)
½ tsp vanilla powder

Place the watermelon and strawberry pieces in a serving bowl. Open the passion fruits and scoop out the pulp over the watermelon and strawberry. Drizzle the lime juice on top.

To make the dressing, in a small bowl mix the yogurt, maple syrup, and vanilla powder. Serve with the fruit salad.

Tip! For a more filling salad, add mozzarella or vegan mozzarella.

Wellness

Pampering Foot Soaks

These mini summer spa treatments for your feet are easily made from common ingredients. Depending on your mood, try one of these combination. Assemble the foot soaks using the ratio of 2 cups of plants to 1 gallon (4 l) of water.

FOREST SPA

Refreshes and relaxes tired and numb legs after a long day or if you have a cold.

1 cup (14oz/400 g) Epsom salt
1 cup birch leaves
½ cup pine needles
½ cup meadowsweet flowers or
    peppermint leaves
1 gallon (4 l) water, hot

SUMMERNIGHT'S DREAM SOAK

Revitalizes, disinfects, and treats muscle pain and inflammation.

1 cup (14oz/400 g) Epsom salt
3 tbsp baking soda
1 cup lady's mantle (or clover leaves)
½ cup plantain leaves (or holy basil)
½ cup common yarrow flowers
    (or chamomile flowers)
1 gallon (4 l) water, hot

Add the plants into a footbath bowl. Pour hot water and steep for about 15 minutes. Place your feet in the water and enjoy the footbath for about 15 minutes. Dry your feet thoroughly.

Floral Smudge Sticks

The tradition of making smudge sticks from herbs has been used in different cultures, ceremonies, and rituals. Gathering herbs, tying them into bundles, and then burning them is a pleasant meditative experience. I like to collect flowers during the Midsummer celebration in early summer (as it's said to be a magical time), create an intention, and then burn the smudge sticks later in the summer.

INGREDIENT SUGGESTIONS

Sage, rosemary, lavender, dill, mugwort, dandelion, wild rose petals, peyoni petals, marigold, lemon verbena, peppermint, pine sprig, catnip, basil, chamomile, thyme

Cut the herbs (or plants or flowers) into pieces that are 4–6 inches (10–15 cm) long and trim the stems to the same length. Spread and overlap the herbs on a flat surface to create a mat and then roll into a tight bundle. Cut a piece of string to about 28 inches (70 cm) and tie the string firmly to the base of the bundle. If you use flower petals, roll them last onto the surface of the bundle. Twist the string tightly around the bundle toward the top. Once you reach the top of the bundle, circle back and towards the bundle's base. Tie tightly. Leave to dry for 4–5 days.

Light the top of the smudge stick and move it around in the air for a moment to spread its scent. Begin by only burning a small amount so that the intensity of the scent does not come as a surprise. Be sure to completely extinguish the smudge stick and check that it is not smoldering before storing it.

Honey Face Masks

One of my favorite DIY face masks uses local organic honey, which is a brilliant skin remedy. It has soothing, moisturizing, exfoliating, and antibacterial properties. It is naturally suited for many skin types but can be easily customized.

HIGH MOISTURE MASK
For dry and thirsty skin.

1 tbsp local organic honey
½ avocado, pitted and peeled

GLOW MASK
For impurities and dull skin.

1 tbsp local organic honey
½ tsp ground turmeric

EXFOLIATING MASK
Helps remove dead skin cells.

1 tbsp local organic honey
1 tbsp rolled oats

Mix the ingredients, apply to your face, and let sit for 15–20 minutes. Use a warm washcloth to wipe off.

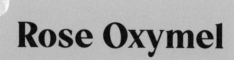

Rose Oxymel

Oxymel, also known as sour honey,
comes from ancient Greece. It is a
therapeutic composition used in natural medicine
and is made by mixing vinegar, honey, and herbs.

Oxymel is *also believed to strengthen immunity, treat sore throats, and help digestive problems, among other things. Rose oxymel is said to bring harmony and feminine strength–and it also makes for an interesting salad dressing! Add 1 teaspoon of the mixture to a warm drink, or take a spoonful if you feel a cold coming or need some immune system reinforcement. You can also add it to sparkly drinks or enjoy it with bread or salad.*

½ cup (approx. 20) wild rose petals
½ cup (4 fl oz/120 ml) apple cider vinegar
¼ cup (2½ oz/70 g) local organic honey

Add all the ingredients into a sealable glass jar. Mix them together and close the jar tightly. Move the jar to a cool, dark place and leave to infuse for 2 weeks. Shake the jar briskly a couple of times a week. After 2 weeks, strain the petals from the mixture. Keep oxymel in a closed glass jar in the refrigerator, where it can be stored for 6 months.

Note! Do not give oxymel and honey to children under the age of 1.

Tip! Try rosemary, thyme, oregano, stinging nettle, garlic, or basil in your oxymel instead of rose petals.

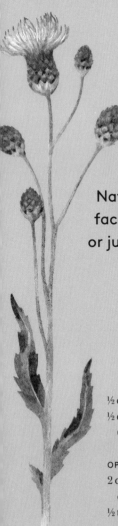

Floral Face Mists

Nature is full of brilliant ingredients for creating nurturing face mists. Whether you harvest fresh plants and dry them or just simply use dried plants, use the ratio of 2 tablespoons of dry plants to ½ cup (4 fl oz/120 ml) of water.

½ cup fresh wild herbs and flowers
½ cup (4 fl oz/120 ml) spring water
   (or rain water or tap water)

OPTIONAL
2 drops almond oil (or jojoba oil), for
   extra moisture
½ tsp apple cider vinegar, for renewing
   skin and minimizing pores

Measure the flowers and herbs into a glass jar. Boil the water and pour into the jar on top of the plants. Leave to infuse for 1 hour or overnight at room temperature, covered from the light. Strain the plants and flowers from the liquid and add almond oil or apple cider vinegar, if desired. Store in a glass jar or spray bottle in the refrigerator and use within a week. Shake before use.

Note! Always test the face mist on a small area of skin first to see if your skin is sensitive or reacts to any allergies.

Tip! Wild herbs are mainly suitable for all skin types, but they also have special qualities. Try out the plants on the next page and find your own favorite. Also, while waiting for the floral face mist ingredients to infuse, try the Botanical Facial Steams on page 161.

Wild rose petals:

Moisturizes and soothes; good for sensitive, dry, and mature skin.

Raspberry leaves:

Softens and tightens the skin, especially irritated or combination skin.

Red clover flowers:

Soothes and softens, especially dry and sensitive skin.

Yarrow flowers:

Shrinks pores and treats inflammation, especially inflamed skin with impurities.

Stinging nettle leaves:

Strengthens and calms; good for sensitive or irritated skin and skin with impurities.

Lady's mantle:

Firms and softens the skin and shrinks pores; good for mature skin or enlarged skin pores.

Birch leaves:

Soothes, calms, and refreshes, especially dry skin or skin with impurities.

Plantain leaves:

Cleans and calms; good for inflamed or acne-prone skin.

Meadowsweet:

Good for inflammation, acne, and redness.

Honeysuckle:

Moisturizes, shrinks pores, and controls inflammation; good for dry skin and skin with impurities.

Marigold flowers:

Soothes and softens; good for sensitive skin.

Sage:

Refreshes and calms inflammation, especially irritated and mature skin.

Mint:

Moisturizes, brightens, and soothes, especially irritated and mature skin.

Rosemary:

Moisturizes, cleanses, and balances, especially combination or inflamed skin.

Vanelja's Rose Mist

Although I love experimenting with different herbs and flowers to use in my face mists, this recipe is my absolute favorite. It leaves my skin feeling incredibly soft and calm and is perfect for sensitive, reactive, dry, and mature skin.

¼ cup (approx. 10) rose petals
¼ cup sage leaves
½ cup (4 fl oz/120 ml) spring water
   (or rain water or tap water)
2 drops jojoba oil
2 drops frankincense essential oil

Measure the rose petals and sage into a glass jar. Boil the water and pour into the jar on top of the plants. Leave to infuse for 3 hours or overnight at room temperature, covered from the light. Strain the plants from the liquid and add the jojoba and frankincense oils. Stir well. Store in a glass jar or spray bottle in the refrigerator and use within a week. Shake before using.

Tip! You can create different kinds of floral face mists by substituting the rose petals for chamomile flowers or lavender flowers. Experiment to find your favorite! Also try herbal teas, such as chamomile tea. Open the tea bag and soak the tea in the water for 1 hour.

Stinging Nettle Hair Rinse

Stinging nettle makes an excellent strengthening hair treatment, which is basically nettle tea that you apply to your hair. It is perfect for maintaining good scalp health and makes your hair soft and shiny.

34 ounces (1 l) water
2 cups (2 oz/60 g) fresh stinging nettle
2 tbsp other herbs, such as rosemary,
    lavender, or sage (optional)

Measure the water into a large saucepan and bring to a boil. Take off the heat and add the stinging nettle and additional herbs, if using. Cover the pan and allow it to infuse for 5 hours or overnight. Strain out the herbs.

Shampoo your hair as usual. Pour about ½ cup (4 fl oz/120 ml) over wet hair and massage into your scalp and hair for a couple of minutes. Rinse with water. Use once a week. Store in the refrigerator and use within 1–2 weeks.

Note! If your hair is light colored, this rinse might color it. You can substitute the stinging nettle leaves with 2–4 tablespoons of another herb, such as chamomile, lavender, parsley, rosemary, peppermint, thyme, or sage. Try different herbs and find the ones that condition your hair and scalp best. If you have an itchy scalp or dandruff, stir in 1 tablespoon of apple cider vinegar.

Botanical Facial Steams

Homemade facial steams made with herbs and wildflowers are heavenly spa treatments and a beautiful way to relax—plus they leave your skin looking fresh and smooth.

Additional benefits *of a facial steam are that it opens the pores and removes dirt and impurities; increases circulation to help skin glow and look firmer; naturally moisturizes and hydrates your skin; helps skin products and moisturizers absorb deeper into skin; and relaxes your body and mind to destress!*

2–4 cups (475–950 ml) pure water, such as rain water, spring water, or tap water

¼ cup fresh herbs and flowers (or 2 tbsp dried herbs and flowers)

2–5 drops essential oil, such as lavender, frankincense, rose, lemon, or chamomile (optional)

Heat the water until it simmers. Pour the water into a large bowl and stir in the herbs and flowers. Add essential oils, if desired. Tie your hair back and drape a towel over your head so that it creates a tent. Hold your face over the steam and enjoy for about 10 minutes. Close your eyes and breathe deeply. Be careful to protect your skin; do not get too close to the water or steam for too long. Pat your skin dry and apply your favorite moisturizer.

Tip! Check out the list of herbs and flowers and their benefits on page 157.

Note! If your skin is very sensitive, try face steaming gently with a mild steam and only for a couple of minutes to see how your skin likes it.

Body Glow Oil

This is my go-to natural self-tanner for the body. It's super easy to make, it gives your skin a beautiful golden tone, and it smells like divine cacao. Vary the amount of cacao powder, depending on your skin tone. The color will rinse away when you shower.

¼ cup (2 fl oz/60 ml) mild-flavored coconut oil (or jojoba oil or almond oil)
2–5 tsp cacao powder

Melt the coconut oil in a bain-marie if it's hard. Pour into a small jar and add the cacao powder. Stir well. Pour into a small jar or bottle. A small pump bottle works well, but a spray bottle won't let the mixture through. Spread evenly onto the skin and rub it well with your hands. Let dry fully before putting on your clothes so that they don't get stained.

Note! I always use coconut oil that says "mild flavor" on the label so that the fragrance is nice and subtle. Something to try if you're not a fan of coconut scent.

Tip! Try using coffee as a natural fake tan. Stir 2–3 tbsp of instant coffee and ¼ cup (2 fl oz/60 ml) baby lotion together in a bowl. Use it as a bronzer and spread it on your skin.

Acknowledgments

I want to thank you, dear reader, for joining me throughout these tasty summer adventures. I hope this book will bring a lot of joy and delight to your summer. You are the reason I do this work, and I thank you. Thank you to my love pack, Alva, Finn, and Helle, for the best summer adventures. Thank you to my parents and family for everything we've experienced during the summers in our northern homestead. Thank you, Pirjo and Matts, for the magical world of Åland and its delicacies. Thank you, my friends; you make my summers unforgettable. And finally, thank you, Mother Nature, for all your treasures and gifts; I am forever grateful.

About the Author

Virpi Mikkonen is a recipe artist, author, and an ambassador for natural well-being living in Helsinki, Finland. She has twelve years of experience in the wellness field and holds degrees in journalism and health coaching. Her Instagram account, Vanelja, was chosen to be included in Instagram's Suggested Users list and is well known among foodies around the world. Her website, Vanelja.com, was awarded the Saveur Food Blog Award, as well as Finnish blog awards. *Full Bloom* is Virpi's fifth book.

WORKS CONSULTED

Holmberg, Pelle; Eklöf, Marie-Louise; Pedersen, Anders; Vainio, Hannele. *Mauste- ja lääkekasvit luonnossa*; Otava, 2009

Kress, Henriette. *Käytännön lääkekasvit*; Yrtit ja yrttiterapia Henriette Kress, 2010

Piippo, Sinikka. *Elinvoimaa mausteista*; Minerva Kustannus, 2015

Piippo, Sinikka. *Kasvien salaiset voimat*; Helmi Kustannus, 2008

Vermasheinä, Kaisa. *Lempeää kauneutta luonnosta*; Kirjapaja, 2016

Index

A WELDON OWEN PRODUCTION
PO Box 3088
San Rafael, CA 94912
www.weldonowen.com

NewSeed Press
is an imprint of Weldon Owen International

NewSeed Press would like to thank Jessica Easto and Timothy Griffin
for their contributions.

Printed in China

10 9 8 7 6 5 4 3 2 1

ISBN: 978-1-68188-872-9

WELDON OWEN INTERNATIONAL
CEO: Raoul Goff
Publisher: Roger Shaw
Editorial Director: Katie Killebrew
Senior Editor: John Foster
Production Manager: Sam Taylor